Full Sails

Senior Authors

Roger C. Farr

Dorothy S. Strickland

Authors

Richard F. Abrahamson ♦ Alma Flor Ada ♦ Barbara Bowen Coulter
Bernice E. Cullinan ♦ Margaret A. Gallego
W. Dorsey Hammond
Nancy Roser ♦ Junko Yokota ♦ Hallie Kay Yopp

Senior Consultant

Asa G. Hilliard III

Consultants

Lee Bennett Hopkins ♦ Stephen Krashen ♦ David A. Monti ♦ Rosalia Salinas

Harcourt Brace & Company

Orlando Atlanta Austin Boston San Francisco Chicago Dallas New York Toronto London

ISBN 0-15-310812-6

4 5 6 7 8 9 10   048   2000 99

Dear Reader,

You will find many adventures in this book. Follow Henny Penny into Foxy Loxy's cave, but watch out! Sail the ocean with Jenny, and make friends with some dolphins. Read rhymes from China, the Rio Grande, and other places in the world.

There are so many adventures to share when you read. Set sail into a world of fun!

Sincerely,

The Authors

Story Tellers

ONE AND ALL

CONTENTS

Where the Green Grass Grows

CONTENTS

CONTENTS

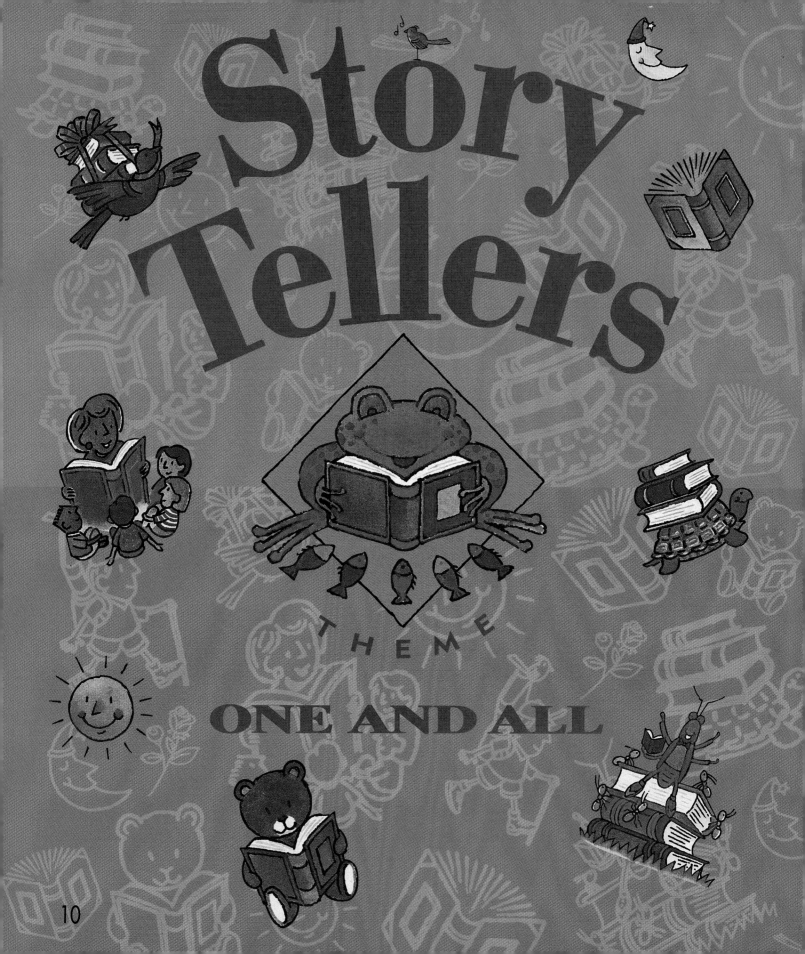

Story Tellers

THEME

ONE AND ALL

Many people like stories, folktales, and rhymes. Come along and meet some happy hens and a very brave egg. You will also meet some storytellers along the way.

CONTENTS

11

Bookshelf

One warm spring morning, Millie was skipping around in her field, feeling happy. She sniffed a yellow flower and almost sat on a bird.

Three Bags Full

Story by
Ragnhild Scamell
Pictures by
Sally Hobson

Three Bags Full
by Ragnhild Scamell

Milly is happy to share her wool
with three of her friends. But silly Milly
forgets to keep some for herself!

Signatures Library

The Ugly Little Duck
by Patricia and Fredrick McKissack

Poor Little Duck is not very happy. Then he learns something about himself that changes everything.

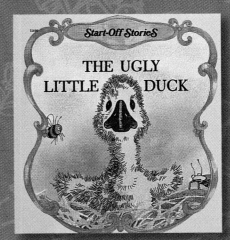

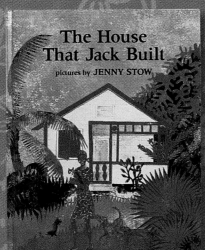

The House That Jack Built
by Jenny Stow

An old story is told in a new way. This time Jack's house is by the sea.

The Three Bears
by Byron Barton

The three bears come home to find that things are not the same! What has Goldilocks done this time?

14

The Little Red Hen

Byron Barton

Award-Winning
Author/Illustrator

The Little Red Hen
Byron Barton

Once there were four friends—

a pig,

a duck,

a cat,

and a little red hen.

The little red hen had three baby chicks.

One day the little red hen
was pecking in the ground,
and she found some seeds.

17

She went to her three friends and asked,
"Who will help me plant these seeds?"

"Not I," squealed the pig.
"Not I," quacked the duck.
"Not I," meowed the cat.

"Then I will plant the seeds,"
said the little red hen.

And she did.

And the seeds sprouted and grew
into large stalks of wheat.

Then the little red hen asked her three friends,
"Who will help me cut these stalks of wheat?"

"Not I," meowed the cat.
"Not I," squealed the pig.
"Not I," quacked the duck.

"Then I will cut the wheat,"
said the little red hen.

And she did.

Then the little red hen asked her friends,
"Who will help me thresh this wheat?"

"Not I," squealed the pig.
"Not I," quacked the duck.
"Not I," meowed the cat.

"Then I will thresh the wheat,"
said the little red hen.

And she did.

Then the little red hen asked
her friends, "Who will help
me grind these grains of
wheat into flour?"

"Not I," squealed the pig.
"Not I," quacked the duck.
"Not I," meowed the cat.

"Then I will grind the wheat into flour,"
said the little red hen.

And she did.

Then the little red hen asked her three friends,
"Who will help me make this flour into bread?"

"Not I," meowed the cat.
"Not I," squealed the pig.
"Not I," quacked the duck.

"Then I will make the flour
into bread," she said.

And she did.

Then the little red hen called to her friends,
"Who will help me eat this bread?"

"I will," quacked the duck.
"I will," meowed the cat.
"I will," squealed the pig.

"Oh no," said the little red hen.
"We will eat the bread."

And they did—

the little red hen and her three little chicks.

· Byron Barton ·

Do you like to paint? When Byron Barton was a boy, he loved to paint. One time Byron's family moved, and he went to a new school. The work was too easy for him there, so the teacher let him paint. She hung up his pictures, and his friends called him "the artist."

When Byron Barton grew up, he got married. His wife made picture books. Soon he wanted to try it, too. "Now I am doing picture books all the time," he says.

GOOD BOOKS

Good books.
Good times.
Good stories.
Good rhymes.
Good beginnings.
Good ends.
Good people.
Good friends.

GOOD TIMES

Good fiction.
Good facts.
Good adventures.
Good acts.
Good stories.
Good rhymes.
Good books.
Good times.

by Lee Bennett Hopkins
illustrated by Linda Solovic

Make a Shape Book

Everyone can help make this bread! Pretend that you are in the story "The Little Red Hen." Write about what you will do to help.

You will need:
a bread tracer   paper
crayons   scissors
tape

36

After your bread is made, write a sentence telling how you will help the Little Red Hen. Draw a picture to go with your sentence.

We will help the Little Red Hen!

Patty will help plant the seeds.

Sandra will help cut the wheat.

David will help bake the bread.

Put all the pages together to make a book.

Everyone can help read the shape book.

You can read your page and act out how you would help.

We will help the Little Red Hen!

HENNY

PENNY

adapted from
a retelling by Stephen Butler

CHARACTERS

Narrator	Henny Penny
Goosey Loosey	Cocky Locky
Ducky Lucky	Turkey Lurkey
	Foxy Loxy

Narrator: One day while Henny Penny was sitting beneath the oak tree an acorn fell and hit her on the head.

Henny Penny: Goodness me! The sky is falling! I must go and tell the king.

Narrator: So Henny Penny ran off in a great hurry to tell the king the sky was falling. She had not gone far before she met Cocky Locky.

Cocky Locky: Where are you
going, Henny Penny?

Henny Penny: Oh, Cocky Locky! The sky is falling!
And I am going to tell the king.

Cocky Locky: Goodness me! I'll come with you.

Narrator: So Henny Penny and Cocky Locky hurried on
to tell the king the sky was falling. They had not gone
far before they met Ducky Lucky.

Ducky Lucky: Where are you two going?

Cocky Locky: Oh, Ducky Lucky! The sky is falling! And we are going to tell the king.

Ducky Lucky: Goodness me! I'll come with you.

Narrator: So Henny Penny, Cocky Locky, and Ducky Lucky hurried on to tell the king the sky was falling. They had not gone far before they met Goosey Loosey.

Goosey Loosey: Where are you all going?

Ducky Lucky: Oh, Goosey Loosey! The sky is falling!
And we are going to tell the king.

Goosey Loosey: Goodness me! I'll come with you.

Narrator: So Henny Penny, Cocky Locky,
Ducky Lucky, and Goosey Loosey hurried on to
tell the king the sky was falling. They had not
gone far before they met Turkey Lurkey.

Turkey Lurkey: Where are you all going?

Goosey Loosey: Oh, Turkey Lurkey! The sky is falling! And we are going to tell the king.

Turkey Lurkey: Goodness me! I'll come with you.

Narrator: So Henny Penny, Cocky Locky, Ducky Lucky, Goosey Loosey, and Turkey Lurkey hurried on to tell the king the sky was falling. Suddenly Foxy Loxy appeared.

Foxy Loxy: And where are you all going in such a hurry?

All Birds: Oh, Foxy Loxy! The sky is falling! We are going to tell the king.

Foxy Loxy: But you're going the wrong way! The king's palace is *that* way.

Narrator: Foxy Loxy pointed to a path leading into the woods. So Henny Penny, Cocky Locky, Ducky Lucky, Goosey Loosey, and Turkey Lurkey hurried down the path. They ran on and on until at last they reached the king's palace.

47

Foxy Loxy: Come in and tell me your story, Henny Penny.

Narrator: But as Henny Penny curtsied, she saw a bushy red tail beneath the king's robe.

Henny Penny: It's a trap! Run!

Narrator: Foxy Loxy threw off his cunning disguise and sprang to the door.

Foxy Loxy: Surprise! I'm going to eat you all for dinner.

Narrator: Henny Penny woke up with a start and opened her eyes. She was still trembling.

Henny Penny: Goodness me! I must have been dreaming.

Narrator: But just then an acorn fell and hit her on the head.

Henny Penny: Goodness me! The sky is falling! I must go and tell the king.

STEPHEN

Stephen Butler grew up on a farm.
Lots of hens, chicks, and birds
like us lived there.

Stephen and his brother
watched chicks hatch from eggs.

**Watching the farm birds helped me
draw the pictures for *Henny Penny*!**

BUTLER

Now Stephen Butler has a pet tortoise named Sampson. Maybe he will write a story about tortoises!

Let's Make Puppets!

Look at the birds and the fox in "Henny Penny." Choose one to make as a puppet.

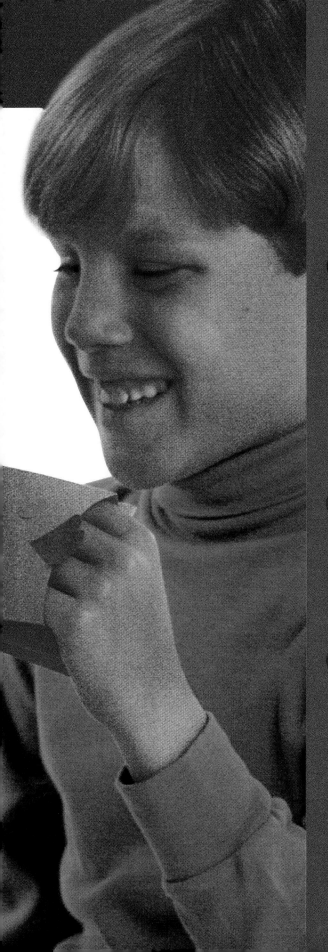

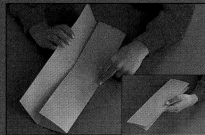 

1. First, fold a sheet of paper like this. **2.** Then, fold the paper in half.

3. Next, fold one side up. Turn the paper over and fold the other side up.

4. Draw or glue on other parts.

5. Slip your thumb and fingers in the slots. Your puppet is done!

When your puppets are finished you can have a puppet show.

A WORLD OF RHYMES

Come and see!
Come and see!
A black hen has laid
A white egg for me!

Traditional Chinese Rhyme

We are little mice

Out to dance and play.

We hope the cat of Don Tomás

Will not come our way.

Traditional Rhyme from the Rio Grande

Little hen upon the wall,

There you peck for wheat grains small;

Pick, pick, peck;

Pick, peck, pay!

Flop your tail and fly away!

Traditional French Rhyme

Humpty Dumpty sat on a wall,
Humpty Dumpty had a great fall;
All the King's horses and all the King's men
Couldn't put Humpty together again.

Traditional English Rhyme

LUMPTY

by MIKO IMAI

LITTLE
LUMPTY

by
MIKO
IMAI

In the little town of Dumpty there was a high wall.
Humpty Dumpty had fallen from it long, long ago.
But people still remembered him.

Every day children played by the wall and sang,
"Humpty Dumpty sat on the wall.
Humpty Dumpty had a great fall."

Little Lumpty loved the wall and always
dreamed about climbing to the top.
"Don't ever do that," Lumpty's mother said.
"Remember, all the king's horses and all the king's
men couldn't put Humpty Dumpty together again."

But Lumpty couldn't stop thinking about the wall. One day on his way home from school, he found a long ladder and dragged it over there.

He climbed up . . . and up . . . and up.

At last he reached the top. "Oh, there's my house!
And there's my school! I can almost touch the clouds!"

Lumpty was so happy that he danced along
like a tightrope walker.
"If only my friends could see me now!"

But then Lumpty looked down. IT WAS A BIG

MISTAKE. His legs began to shake and tremble.

"Oh, no! I don't think I can get back to the ladder.
What if I'm not home by dinnertime?"
It was getting dark and the birds were flying home
to their nests, but still Lumpty could not move.
Suddenly he remembered Humpty Dumpty's great fall.

72

"Help! Help!" Lumpty screamed.

Everyone in town rushed outside to see what was wrong.

"How can we save him?" asked an old man.
"We need a big blanket!" said Lumpty's mother,
and she ran home to get one.

They stretched it out at the bottom of the wall.
"Jump, Lumpty, jump!
Jump, Lumpty, jump!"

Lumpty took a deep breath and
threw himself into the dark night air.

He bounced once,

twice,

three times,

and then came safely to rest on the blanket.

"Mommy, I'm sorry. I just had to see what it would be like on top."

He was so glad to be home.

"But I still love that wall," he whispered to the moon just before he fell asleep.

MIKO IMAI

Miko Imai grew up in Japan. She first heard about Humpty Dumpty when she came to the United States to study painting. "I wanted to save Humpty Dumpty in my paintings," says Miko Imai. "*Little Lumpty* is my first children's book. This time the egg comes through without a crack!"

Lumpty and Miko Imai both like to try new things. "Even though you might have some trouble along the way, it's still great to explore," says Miko Imai.

Miko Imai

83

DUMPTY TOWN NEWS

Volume Number 9

Issue 1

When Little Lumpty got stuck on the wall, it was big news! Your class can write a news story about it for the Dumpty Town Newspaper.

Dumpty Town News
Thursday, January 15, 1998

Little Lumpty Jumps!

Friday night the town heard someone yell "Help!" Everyone

•Make your paper look like a newspaper.
•Write the name and date.
•Draw a picture and write a news story.

Later, you can

- write more news stories for the Dumpty Town News.
- hang your newspaper story in the hallway.

Walk in the woods,

squirm with a worm,

and grow

a garden with

Frog and Toad.

Come out and learn

about the world!

Where the Green

CONTENTS

Grass Grows

Peeping and Sleeping
by Fran Manushkin

Barry and his father take a walk at night to find out what is making strange peeping sounds.

SIGNATURES LIBRARY

Mole's Hill
by Lois Ehlert

Mole loves to dig near the pond. So when the animals of the forest want Mole to leave, she has to think fast!

Ten Flashing Fireflies
by Philemon Sturges

"What do we see on a summer night? Ten flashing fireflies burning bright."

The Four Elements—Earth
by Carme Solé Vendrell and J. M. Parramón

Read about a place where we all live.

89

The WILD

The WILD WOODS

Award-Winning
Author/Illustrator

Simon James

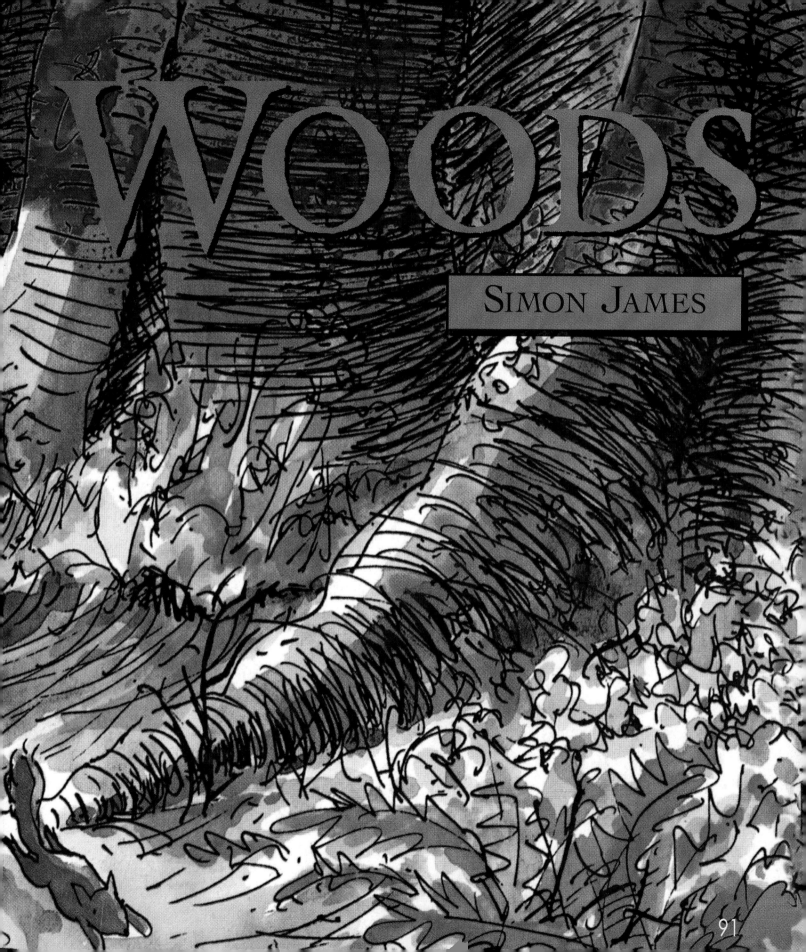

WOODS

SIMON JAMES

Jess was walking with her grandad
when they saw a squirrel.
"I'd like to take him home," Jess said.

"You can't keep a squirrel,"
called Grandad.

"They're too wild."

"I'll take care of him," Jess said. "But you can't keep a squirrel," called Grandad. "What are you going to feed him?"

"He likes our sandwiches,"
Jess said.

"You can't keep a squirrel," shouted Grandad.

"Where's he going to sleep?"

"I'll make him a bed in my room," Jess said.

"Hurry up, Grandad.
I think I found a waterfall."

"You can't really keep a squirrel,"
Grandad whispered.

"I know," said Jess.

"He belongs in the wild."

"I like being in the wild," Jess said.

"Can we come back tomorrow?"

"Well . . . okay," said Grandad.

"Good," Jess said, "because . . ."

 "one of those ducks might need
taking care of."

SIMON JAMES

When Simon James was in school, he enjoyed drawing silly pictures. He always said he wanted to be an artist when he grew up.

When he got out of school, he didn't become an artist right away. There were many other jobs he wanted to try. He worked as a police officer, a farmer, and a store clerk. Simon James tried fourteen different jobs before he decided he really wanted to be an artist and a writer.

Now Simon James spends much of his time writing children's books and teaching art to school children.

RESPONSE CORNER

Have a Sing-Along

Jess and Grandad see lots of things when they walk through the woods. You can make up a song about walking through the woods. Then have a class sing-along.

A-walking we will go.
A-walking we will go.
Look and see _____
As through the woods we go.

Use this sentence to make up a line for the song.
If you'd like to, you can make a picture to go with it.

Look and see **the big brown bear**.

Sing along together.
Sing your line when it's your turn.
Later you can sing for another class.

You know
this furry animal.

It is a

SQUIRREL

Squirrels bury nuts
to eat in the winter.

You can see squirrels
in your backyard.
They love to get into
bird feeders to eat seeds.

You can see squirrels
in the park. Sometimes
squirrels get a drink
from a water fountain.

Most of the time, you see squirrels in a tree.
Here they can stretch out on a branch to rest,
just like this sleepy squirrel is doing.
Have a good nap, squirrel.

WONDERFUL

WONDERFUL
WORMS

BY LINDA GLASER
PICTURES BY
LORETTA KRUPINSKI

WORMS

Earthworms are fat and wiggly
like my fingers and toes.
They live where it is cool and dark and damp,
where roots spread out like underground trees.

Worms feel sounds with their whole bodies.
They feel thunder when I walk.

They are wonderful diggers.
They dig passageways and burrows.
But they don't use shovels or fingers or toes.

How do they do it?
They eat their way through and move along.

They stretch out, long and thin,
and squeeze in, short and fat.
Stretch and squeeze, stretch and squeeze.
Eat and dig, move and dig.

Earthworms mix and turn the dirt
as they dig and tunnel in the earth.
They make the soil soft and airy
so the roots of plants can breathe and grow.

Worms don't have eyes or ears or a nose.
They do have a mouth.
And they need food, just like I do.
But they eat dirt and rotting leaves.

They swallow tiny pieces.
And inside the worms, the food changes.
When it comes out of their tail ends,
it makes the earth rich so plants can grow.

Earthworms are my helpers, the underground gardeners. We work hard in the dirt in my garden, their home.

LINDA GLASER

Linda Glaser lives in Minnesota. There she raises her two girls, writes children's books, and teaches writing. She also works in her garden, where she meets many wonderful worms!

When Linda Glaser was a young girl, she loved to write stories. She dreamed of becoming a writer of children's books. Now that she *is* one, she tells children, "Hold on to your dreams. They *can* come true!"

Linda Glaser

LORETTA KRUPINSKI

Loretta Krupinski lives by a river, a lake, and an ocean. She loves the water and enjoys painting pictures of boats and the ocean.

Do you have a favorite hobby? Drawing is Loretta Krupinski's favorite hobby. She says that to her, drawing is like eating and sleeping. It's so much a part of her life that she does it every day. "I began drawing and painting as a very young child, and I have never stopped," she says.

Loretta Krupinski

The EARTHWORM

Lombriz soterrada
trabaja, trabaja
callada, callada.

An earthworm doesn't
make a sound
when he's working
underground.

by Ernesto Galarza

TOMMY

I put a seed into the ground
And said, "I'll watch it grow."
I watered it and cared for it
As well as I could know.

One day I walked in my back yard,
And oh, what did I see!
My seed had popped itself right out,
Without consulting me.

by Gwendolyn Brooks

Award-Winning
Author

Illustrated by
Dale Verzaal

127

Response Corner

Wonderful Worm Poems

Worms are wonderful!
You saw how they look and how they move.
You can use what you learned to
write a poem about worms.

You will need: worm-shaped paper, paper, glue

1. Write *Worms* on a blue worm.

2. Write two words that tell what worms look like on two orange worms.

3. Write three words that tell what worms do on three yellow worms.

4. Write a good name for a pet worm on a brown worm.

5. Glue the worm colors in the same order you see here.

You can
- write poems about other animals.
- put your poems in a class book.

GARDEN

Some insects
are pests
in gardens.
Others are
garden friends.

FRIENDS

This praying mantis is a garden friend.

Praying mantis

So is the round, red ladybug.

Ladybug

Aphids

Garden friends eat insects
such as aphids (A-fids)
that eat garden plants.

Do you have a garden?

ALA Notable
Book

Newbery
Honor

Frog

Toge

ARNOLD
LOBEL

*Frog and Toad
Together*

by Arnold Lobel

An I CAN READ Book

and Toad
ther

135

The
Garden

Frog was in his garden.
Toad came walking by.
"What a fine garden
you have, Frog," he said.

"Yes," said Frog. "It is very nice,
but it was hard work."

"I wish I had a garden," said Toad.

"Here are some flower seeds.
Plant them in the ground," said Frog,
"and soon you will have a garden."

"How soon?" asked Toad.

"Quite soon," said Frog.

Toad ran home.

He planted the flower seeds.

"Now seeds," said Toad,

"start growing."

Toad walked up and down
a few times.

The seeds did not start to grow.

Toad put his head
close to the ground
and said loudly,
"Now seeds, start growing!"
Toad looked at the ground again.
The seeds did not start to grow.

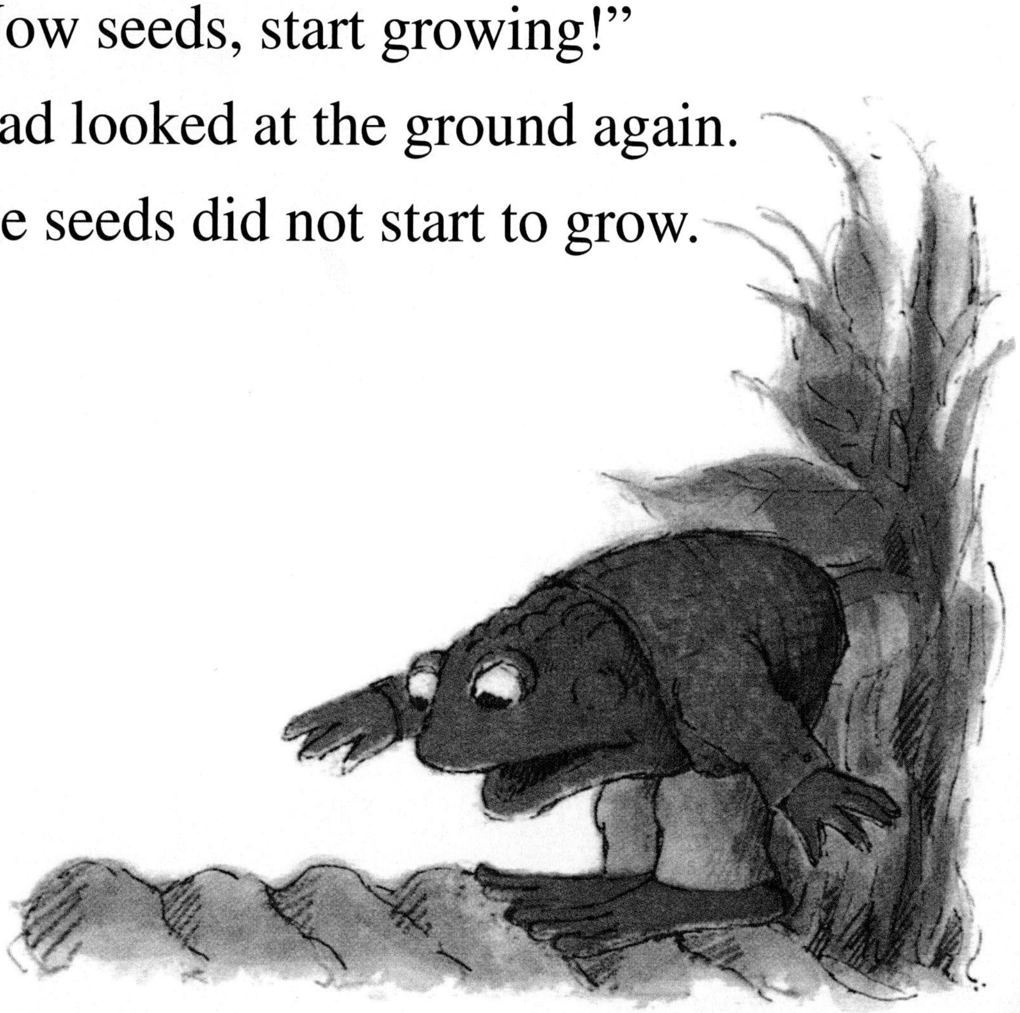

Toad put his head
very close to the ground and shouted,
"NOW SEEDS, START GROWING!"

Frog came running up the path.

"What is all this noise?" he asked.

"My seeds will not grow," said Toad.

"You are shouting too much,"
said Frog. "These poor seeds
are afraid to grow."

"My seeds are afraid to grow?"
asked Toad.

"Of course," said Frog.

"Leave them alone for a few days.

Let the sun shine on them,

let the rain fall on them.

Soon your seeds will start to grow."

That night Toad looked
out of his window.

"Drat!" said Toad.

"My seeds have not
started to grow.

They must be afraid of the dark."

Toad went out to his garden
with some candles.

"I will read the seeds a story," said Toad.

"Then they will not be afraid."

Toad read a long story to his seeds.

All the next day
Toad sang songs
to his seeds.

And all the next day
Toad read poems
to his seeds.

And all the next day
Toad played music
for his seeds.

Toad looked at the ground.
The seeds still did not
start to grow.
"What shall I do?" cried Toad.
"These must be the
most frightened seeds
in the whole world!"
Then Toad felt very tired,
and he fell asleep.

"Toad, Toad, wake up," said Frog.

"Look at your garden!"

Toad looked at his garden.

Little green plants were coming up

out of the ground.

"At last," shouted Toad,

"my seeds have stopped

being afraid to grow!"

"And now you will have
a nice garden too," said Frog.

"Yes," said Toad,

"but you were right, Frog.
It was very hard work."

ARNOLD LOBEL

When Arnold Lobel was a boy, he loved telling stories to his classmates. "I didn't know how the stories were going to end," he said. "The stories just came out of me, and I drew pictures to go with them."

Arnold Lobel wrote many Frog and Toad stories. He got story ideas by watching his children's pet frogs and toads. Maybe you can get story ideas from watching pets, too.

A Talking Flower Play

If the flowers in Toad's garden could talk, what would they say about his shouting, reading, singing, and music playing?

Make a flower mask. Plan what the flowers will say, and then have a play.

construction paper
paper plate
scissors
tape
glue
craft stick

1. Cut out the middle of a paper plate.

2. Make some paper flower petals. Glue them around your plate.

3. Tape a stick to the plate.

Work with a partner. Plan what you will say about Toad.

When you are ready, put on your play for the group. Wear your flower mask and talk in a flower-like voice.

Visit with some snowmen, make an ice castle, and sail the ocean. As you read these stories, think about the fun you can have using your imagination.

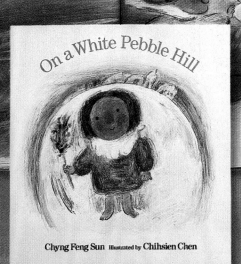

On a White Pebble Hill

by Chyng Feng Sun

Mimi's dinner turns into all kinds of things—
a giant, a snake, a car, a lake, and more.

SIGNATURES LIBRARY

BOOKSHELF

Big Black Bear
by Wong Herbert Yee

Meet a funny bear who needs to learn some manners!

The Trek
by Ann Jonas

Two friends see wild, jungle animals each day as they bravely walk to school.

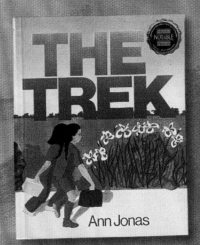

Morton and Sidney
by Chris Demarest

Sidney, Morton's monster friend, gets thrown out of the bedroom closet. What will he and Morton do now?

BY STEPHEN KRENSKY

Lionel in the Winter

PICTURES BY SUSANNA NATTI

Award-Winning
Author and
Illustrator

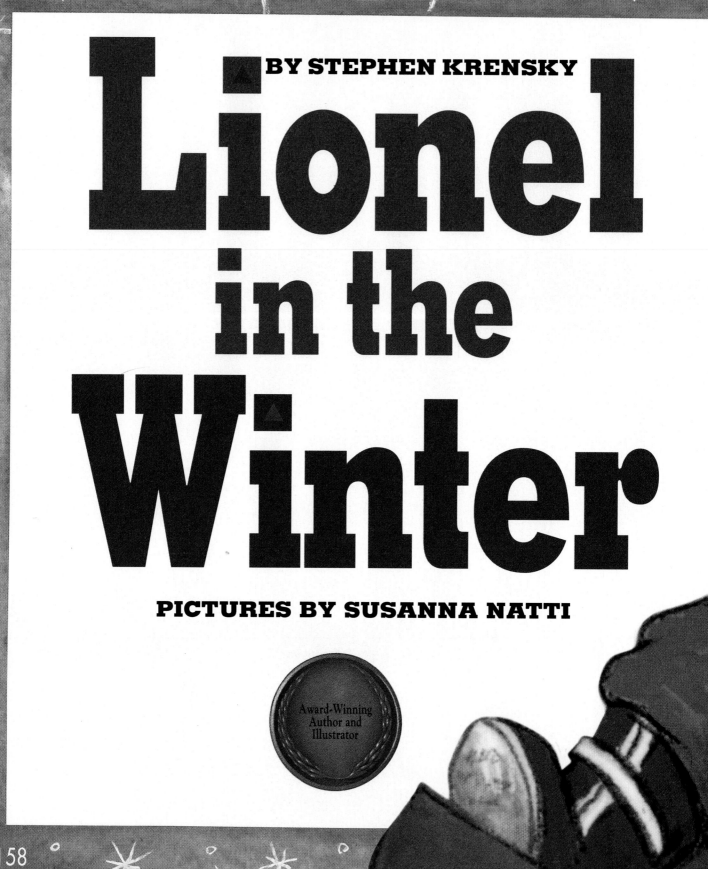

The Snowman

Lionel was building a snowman with his friend Jeffrey.

The snowman was made of three balls of snow.

There was a big ball at the bottom, a medium ball in the middle, and a small ball on top.

Lionel pulled a potato out of his pocket.

"I'll use this for a nose," he said.

"A potato?" said Jeffrey. "Don't most people use carrots?"

"Yes," said Lionel, "but I think more people have noses like potatoes."

Lionel picked up two branches.

"These will be the arms," he said.

"They even have fingers at the end."

"What about the eyes?" Jeffrey asked.

"I brought these two marbles," said Lionel.

He put them in carefully.

Then he added a hat and a scarf.

"Aren't those yours?" asked Jeffrey.

Lionel nodded. "Only the best for
my snowman," he said.

Then he stepped back.

"You know, he looks kind of familiar."

Louise opened the window.

"Lionel!" she yelled out, "you're pointing the snowman the wrong way. He's supposed to face the street."

"That's silly," Lionel yelled back.

"There's nothing for him to look at in the street.

There's a lot more for him to see in our house."

Louise shook her head and shut the window.

"Besides," Lionel said to Jeffrey, "if he's facing

the house, he can help guard it."

"Guard it?" said Jeffrey. "From what?"

Lionel pointed to the fence.

"Maybe tigers," he said.

Jeffrey nodded. "But fighting tigers

could be dangerous," he said.

"You're right," said Lionel.

He ran inside and came out again.

"That's better," he said. Jeffrey shivered.

"Can we go inside soon?" he asked.

"Sure," said Lionel.

He looked at the snowman.

"Do you think he'll be lonely out here by himself?"

"I don't know," said Jeffrey. "But there's nothing we can do about that. We can't bring him inside with us."

"That's true," said Lionel. "But we can still help."
A short time later Lionel and Jeffrey went inside
for cocoa. The snowman stayed outside,
but he wasn't lonely at all.

Stephen Krensky

When Stephen Krensky was a boy, he used to make up stories in bed and try to dream about them. He did not want to be a writer, though. He wanted to be a superhero!

Although Krensky still likes superheroes, he became a writer instead. He says that some stories are easy to do and others take a long time. "Sometimes I write a story from beginning to end. Sometimes I write just a little and add more words until the story is just right."

Stephen Krensky

Susanna Natti

Susanna Natti began drawing when she was five. "I've always liked to draw," she says. "When I was five, I used to try to copy paintings from my parents' art books. By the time I was eight, I knew I was going to be an illustrator. My cousin and I used to have drawing contests. We'd pick a subject, like snow, and then we'd both draw a picture about it."

Susanna Natti

I Am a SNOWM

I am a snowman made of snow.
I stand quite still at ten below,
With a big potato for a nose,
And worn-out shoes to make my toes.

I have two apples for my eyes,
And a woolen coat about this size.
I have a muffler warm and red,
And a funny hat upon my head.

The sun is coming out. Oh, dear!
The sun is melting me, I fear.
Oh, my, I was so nice and round.
Now I'm just a puddle on the ground!

by Louise Binder Scott
Illustrated by Tuko Fujisaki

AN

RESPONSE CORNER

Make a Snowman Town

Lionel and Jeff pretended that their snowmen were guarding the house. Now it's your turn to pretend. Your class can make a town of talking snowmen.

If a snowman could talk, what would he say? Would he talk about the weather? Would he try to make friends? Make a snowman, and write what he will say. Glue on some cotton balls to look like snow.

When you have made your snowman,

- put it in a town with other snowmen.
- read what all the snowmen are saying.
- write a story about the snowman town.

Winter Wonders

by Tanner Ottley Gay

All over the world,
wherever winters are cold,
people make wonderful sculptures—
from snow, ice, and imagination.

Winter sculptures are perfect
for pretending.

How would you like to live
in this ice palace . . .

. . . and have pets like these?

How would you like
to ride this train . . .

. . . or ride this horse . . .

. . . or sail away
on this ship?

The ice sculptures will last
as long as it stays cold.
When it gets warmer, they'll melt away.
Then, next winter, people will make
wonderful new sculptures—
from snow, ice, and imagination!

Jenny's Journey

Sheila White Samton

One day Jenny got a letter from her best friend who had moved far away. Jenny felt sad because her friend was lonely.

Jenny wrote back right away.

Here I come! The sun is rising and I'm setting
out! I'm sailing my boat through the tugboats
and the sailboats and the motorboats
and the ferries,

and past the statue of Our Lady of the Harbor, and under a bridge,

till I get to the open sea!

Maria, I wake up all alone on the ocean!

Remember how lonely I felt when you moved away?
I feel lonely now, too, but then a dolphin shoots out
of the water.

Then another one! And here come some sea gulls!
They all want my breakfast! It's like the day we fed
the seals at the zoo.

"Little girl, little girl,
where are you going?"

"Don't worry,
don't worry.
I'm going
to visit Maria."

I sail along. Suddenly I'm in the shadow of a big, black wall!
It's an ocean liner! Far above my head, a voice booms out.

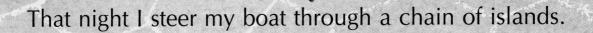

That night I steer my boat through a chain of islands.

When I open my eyes in the morning, *Oh, no!*
I'm caught in a storm at sea! The howling wind fills my sail,
and all day long, I steer up and down waves like mountains,

until the ocean is calm again,
and I can take out my guitar and sing.

"Oh, Maria, don't you cry for me,
for I'm comin' for to see ya,
right across the deep blue sea."

By now you probably think I'll never get there.
But the next day,

I finally see land! There's a long pier
and *you* are on it, waiting for me!

Hooray!

So don't feel lonely.
(And someday I really
will come to see you!)

Love, your friend,

Jenny

SHEILA WHITE SAMTON

Dear Boys and Girls,

My best friend moved away when I was eight. I was very lonely, and I missed my friend a lot. Writing stories and drawing pictures made me feel better. When I was writing or drawing, I forgot that I missed my friend. Have you ever had a friend move away? What did you do to make yourself feel better?

Sheila

Sheila White Samton

♡

By Myself

by Eloise Greenfield

When I'm by myself

And I close my eyes

I'm a twin

I'm a dimple in a chin

I'm a room full of toys

I'm a squeaky noise

I'm a gospel song

I'm a gong

I'm a leaf turning red

I'm a loaf of brown bread

I'm a whatever I want to be

An anything I care to be

And when I open my eyes

What I care to be

Is me

RESPONSE CORNER

Greetings from Maria's Island

Make a postcard to send to a friend. You can show what Maria's island looks like. Then you can write a note to your friend about the island.

Look through books about islands for ideas. Draw an island picture on the front of a card. Write to your friend on the back. After you have made your postcard, plan an island beach party.

You can read your postcards at the party.

Dear Jenny,
This island has lots of palm trees.

Glossary

WHAT IS A GLOSSARY?
A glossary is like a small dictionary. This glossary is here to help you. You can look up a word and then read a sentence that uses that word. Some words have a picture to help you.

A

afraid   Are you **afraid** of bees?

almost   She **almost** got wet when the water was spilled.

alone   When Bob left, I was all **alone.**

along   We went **along** with them because they knew the way.

another   I had to go to **another** school when we moved.

asked   She **asked** her mom for some water.

B

because   I like you **because** you are nice.

C

care   To **care** for the puppy, Dad gave it food and water.

close   You could get hurt if you go **close** to the fire.

D

danced

danced   The children **danced** to the music.

E

end   Go to the **end** of the line.

every   **Every** child in the class got a gift.

F

facing   We were **facing** the screen so we could see the show.

fall   The apple will **fall** into the basket.

feel   I like to **feel** the warm sand on my feet.

felt   Larry **felt** sick, so he went home.

flour   He put a cup of **flour** into the mixing bowl.

found   Billy **found** a ball in the tall grass.

G

good   The show was very **good.**

ground   The **ground** is wet because it rained.

H

help   They will **help** sweep the house.

home   Lee went **home** after school.

I

into   The boy grew **into** a man.

K

keep   I **keep** my toys in a box.

king's   That is the **king's** gold.

L

last   It is summer, so at **last** I can go
swimming.

later   Mia got home **later** than Ernesto.

leaves

leaves   The tree has **leaves.**

live   Fish **live** in the sea.

M

might   I **might** go to the zoo if I have time.

miss   Did you **miss** me when I was away?

morning   I woke up in the **morning.**

most   Tina had the **most** fun at the party.

moved   We **moved** to a new house.

must   Mom said you **must** not be late to
school.

N

night   It was dark last **night.**

oak

O

oak   Acorns are falling from the big **oak** tree.

open   There is no land near the **open** sea.

outside   It is sunny, so Luis is playing **outside.**

P

past We went **past** a house.

plant We will **plant** a garden.

plant

R

right I need the **right** size shoe, or it will not fit.

S

sandwiches He ate two **sandwiches** for lunch.

scarf Kathy has a red **scarf** around her neck.

short That tree is tall, but this one is **short**.

shouted "Hurry back!" she **shouted**.

sky The birds fly up in the blue **sky**.

small The kitten is very **small**.

snow **Snow** is frozen rain.

soft The pillow felt **soft**.

snow

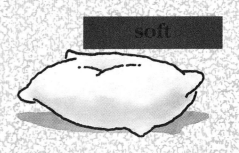
soft

some   Anna read just **some** of her books.

someday   **Someday** Jo will visit us again.

still   I **still** go to the ball games after school.

story   We read a good **story** in class today.

surprise   Chun had a **surprise** party.

T

their   We went to **their** house.

these   **These** are good books!

they   **They** are nice boys and girls.

together   The children sat **together** at lunch.

town   The **town** I live in is very small.

trees   **Trees** need sun to grow.

turn   Please **turn** to the next page.

W

wasn't   **Wasn't** it a hot day?

way   Which **way** do we go to get to the park?

where   I don't know **where** my puppy went.

while   Tenisha likes to sing **while** she is working.

whispered   She **whispered** a secret in my ear.

who   **Who** is that girl?

wild   A **wild** bird is not a pet.

wish   Tasha made a **wish** for a new bicycle.

woke   Ben **woke** up in the morning.

work   They will have to **work** hard.

world   Our **world** is the planet Earth.

wrote   I **wrote** a note to my friend.

woke

Y

you're   Dad said, "**You're** such a big help!"

work

215

Acknowledgments

For permission to reprint copyrighted material, grateful acknowledgment is made to the following sources:

Barron's Educational Series, Inc.: Cover illustration from *the four elements–earth* by Carme Solé Vendrell and J. M. Parramón. © by Parramón Ediciones, S. A.

The Book House for Children: From "Little Hen Upon the Wall" in *Nursery Friends from France,* translated by Olive Beaupré Miller. © by The United Educators, Inc.

Curtis Brown Ltd.: "Good Books, Good Times!" by Lee Bennett Hopkins from *Good Books, Good Times,* selected by Lee Bennett Hopkins. Text copyright © 1985 by Lee Bennett Hopkins. Published by HarperCollins Publishers.

Childrens Press, Inc.: Cover illustration by Peggy Perry Anderson from *The Ugly Little Duck* by Patricia and Fredrick McKissack. Copyright © 1986 by Regensteiner Publishing Enterprises, Inc.

Clarion Books, a Houghton Mifflin Company imprint: Cover illustration by Jennifer Plecas from *Peeping and Sleeping* by Fran Manushkin. Illustration copyright © 1994 by Jennifer Plecas.

T.S. Denison & Company, Inc.: "I Am a Snowman" from *Rhymes for Learning Times* by Louise Binder Scott. Text copyright © 1983 by T. S. Denison & Co., Inc.

Dial Books for Young Readers, a division of Penguin Books USA Inc.: "The Snowman" from *Lionel in the Winter* by Stephen Krensky, illustrated by Susanna Natti. Text copyright © 1994 by Stephen Krensky; illustrations copyright © 1994 by Susanna Natti. Cover illustration from *The House That Jack Built* by Jenny Stow. Illustration copyright © 1992 by Jenny Stow.

Mae Galarza: Untitled poem (Retitled: "The Earthworm") from *Very Very Short Nature Poems/Poemas Pe-que Pe-que Pe-que-ñitos* by Ernesto Galarza.

Greenwillow Books, a division of William Morrow & Company, Inc.: Cover illustration from *The Trek* by Ann Jonas. Copyright © 1985 by Ann Jonas.

Harcourt Brace & Company: Cover illustration from *Mole's Hill* by Lois Ehlert. Copyright © 1994 by Lois Ehlert.

HarperCollins Publishers: The Little Red Hen by Byron Barton. Copyright © 1993 by Byron Barton. Cover illustration from *The Three Bears* by Byron Barton. Copyright © 1991 by Byron Barton. "Tommy" from *Bronzeville Boys and Girls* by Gwendolyn Brooks. Text copyright © 1956 by Gwendolyn Brooks Blakely. "By Myself" from *Honey, I Love* by Eloise Greenfield. Text copyright © 1978 by Eloise Greenfield. "The Garden" from *Frog and Toad Together* by Arnold Lobel. Copyright © 1971, 1972 by Arnold Lobel.

Houghton Mifflin Company: Cover illustration by Chihsien Chen from *On a White Pebble Hill* by Chyng Feng Sun. Illustration copyright © 1994 by Chihsien Chen. Cover illustration from *Big Black Bear* by Wong Herbert Yee. Copyright © 1993 by Wong Herbert Yee.

The Millbrook Press, Inc.: Wonderful Worms by Linda Glaser, illustrated by Loretta Krupinski. Text copyright 1992 by Linda Glaser; illustrations copyright 1992 by Loretta Krupinski.

National Textbook Company: Nonsense rhyme 2 from *Mother Goose on the Rio Grande.* Text copyright © 1977 by National Textbook Company.

National Wildlife Federation: "The Squirrel" from *Your Big Backyard* Magazine, September 1994. Text copyright 1981 by the National Wildlife Federation. "Garden Friends" from *Your Big Backyard* Magazine, March 1995. Text copyright 1980 by the National Wildlife Federation.

North-South Books Inc., New York: Cover illustration by Anna Vojtech from *Ten Flashing Fireflies* by Philemon Sturges. Illustration copyright © 1995 by Anna Vojtech.

Orchard Books, New York: Cover illustration by Sally Hobson from *Three Bags Full* by Ragnhild Scamell. Illustration copyright © 1993 by Sally Hobson.

Philomel Books: "Come and See!" from *Chinese Mother Goose Rhymes,* selected and edited by Robert Wyndham. Text copyright © 1968 by Robert Wyndham.

Simon & Schuster Books for Young Readers, a division of Simon & Schuster: Cover illustration from *Morton and Sidney* by Chris L. Demarest. Copyright © 1987 by Chris L. Demarest.

Sunset Books, Menlo Park, CA 94025: "Let's Make Puppets," adapted from *Children's Crafts: Fun and Creativity for Ages 5-12.* Text copyright © 1976 by Sunset Publishing Corporation.

Tambourine Books, a division of William Morrow & Company, Inc.: Henny Penny retold by Stephen Butler. Copyright © 1991 by Stephen Butler.

Viking Penguin, a division of Penguin Books USA Inc.: Jenny's Journey by Sheila White Samton. Copyright © 1991 by Sheila Samton.

Walker Books Limited, London: Little Lumpty by Miko Imai. © 1994 by Miko Imai. *The Wild Woods* by Simon James. Copyright © 1993 by Simon James. Published in the United States by Candlewick Press, Cambridge, MA.

Photo Credits

Key: (t) top, (b) bottom, (c) center.
Courtesy of Byron Barton, 33; Courtesy of Stephen Butler, 55; Rick Friedman/Black Star/Harcourt Brace & Company, 83, 172, 173; Courtesy of Simon James, 103; J. Griesebieck/Black Star/Harcourt Brace & Company, 124; Tom Sobolik/Black Star/Harcourt Brace & Company, 125, 203; Van Williams, 151

Illustration Credits

Tim Bowers, Cover Art; Darius Detwiler, 4-5; Brenda York, 6-7; Betsy Everitt, 8-9,154-157; Byron Barton, 14-33; Linda Solovic, 34-35; Stephen Butler,38-55; Kathy Lengyel,58-61; Miko Imai, 62-83; Brenda York, 86-89; Simon James, 90-103; Loretta Krupinski, 110-125; Dale Verzaal,126-127; Nan Brooks, 128-129; Arnold Lobel, 134-151; Susanna Natti,158-173; Tuko Fujisaki, 174-175; Sheila White Samton, 184-203; James A. Porter,204-205; Scott Sheidly, 206-207